How to use this book 

Follow the advice, in italics, where given.
Support the children as they read the text that is shaded in cream.
***Praise** the children at every step!*
Detailed guidance is provided in the Read Write Inc. Phonics Handbook.
Activity 8 (Answer the 'questions to read and answer') only appears in Sets 4–7.

8 reading activities

Children:

1 Practise reading the speed sounds.
2 Read the green and red words for the non-fiction text.
3 Listen as you read the introduction.
4 Discuss the vocabulary check with you.
5 Read the non-fiction text.
6 Re-read the non-fiction text and discuss the 'questions to talk about'.
7 Re-read the non-fiction text with fluency and expression.
9 Practise reading the speed words.

Speed sounds

Consonants *Say the pure sounds (do not add 'uh').*

f	l ll	m	n	r	s	v ve	z s	**sh**	**th**	ng **nk**

b	c k ck	d	g	h	j	p	qu	t	w wh	x	y	ch **tch**

Vowels *Say the vowel sound and then the word, e.g. 'a', 'at'.*

at	hen	in	on	up	day	see	high	blow	zoo

*Each box contains one sound but sometimes more than one grapheme. Focus graphemes are **circled**.*

Green words

Read in Fred Talk (pure sounds).

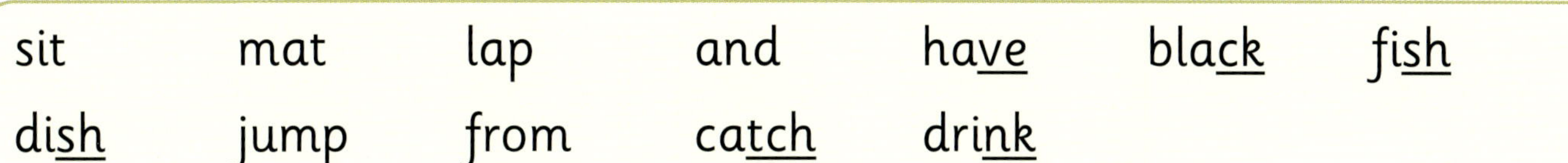

Read the root word first and then with the ending.

leg → legs

moth → moths

Red words

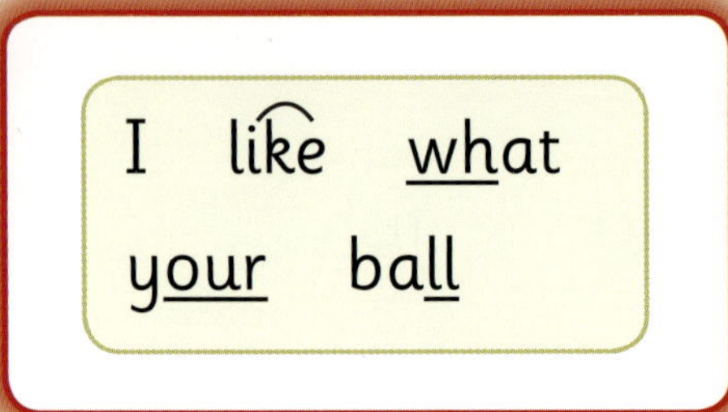

What am I?

Remind children of difference between fiction + non-fiction

Introduction

Have you ever played a guessing game or answered a riddle? At the beginning of this book you will be given some clues and you must try to guess the answer. Good luck!

Written by Gill Munton

Vocabulary check

Discuss the meaning (as used in the non-fiction text) after the children have read the word.

	definition
moths	*tiny insects with wings like butterflies*

Punctuation to note:

I What	*Capital letters that start sentences*
.	*Full stop at the end of each sentence*
?	*Question mark*
!	*Exclamation mark*
...	*'Wait and see' dots*

I have got 4 legs.

I like fish.

What animal do you think it could be?

What am I?

I am a cat!

I am a big black cat!

I can run.
I can jump.
What else might the cat be able to do? eg swim?

I can catch a ball.

I can catch moths.

I can drink milk from a dish.

I can sit on a mat ...

... and I can sit on your lap!
Why would a cat sit on your lap?

Questions to talk about

FIND IT

- ✓ *Turn to the page*
- ✓ *Read the question*
- ✓ *Find the answer*

Page 9:	*What does the cat like to eat?*
Page 11:	*What can the cat do?*
Page 13:	*What else can the cat do?*
Page 14:	*What can the cat drink?*

Speed words

Children practise reading the words across the rows, down the columns and in and out of order clearly and quickly.

sit	jump	leg	can	ball
fish	dish	from	drink	catch
have	milk	run	got	and
big	on	black	lap	mat